What if I Were My Dog and My Dog Were Me?

A PANDEMIC INSPIRED LEARNING TOOL FOR YOUR FAMILY!

Margaret Van Fleet

Balboa Press books may be ordered through booksellers or by contacting:

Balboa Press
A Division of Hay House
1663 Liberty Drive
Bloomington, IN 47403
www.balboapress.com
844-682-1282

ISBN: 978-1-9822-7407-8 (sc)
978-1-9822-7408-5 (e)

Library of Congress Control Number: 2021918574

Print information available on the last page.

Balboa Press rev. date: 02/08/2022

BALBOA.PRESS
A DIVISION OF HAY HOUSE

Preface

This book is written to support parents and teachers in the middle of the 2020 pandemic and to support learning at home organically. My hope is that it will bring families together and develop a great love for writing in learning for children, parents, and teachers globally.

Margaret

What if I were my dog and my dog were me? Would he think of me when I am at work like I do now?

Would he rush to daycare to make sure that I am not the last dog to be picked up from daycare? What would it be like if Shazam was me and if I were him?

I know that I love him the most in the world and he watches every move I make,

and he asks for rubs and gives the best kisses.

What if I were my dog
and my dog were me?

He hops up on the bed and sleeps so easy and feels so peaceful

and then the wind blows by the door then he goes ballistic to kill the wind.

What would I do? Would I fight the wind for him; he does for me?

Does he know that my days are long, and I regret that I can't walk him longer or rub him more?

Did he forgive me like I do him when there were messages left in the middle of the night behind the door?

What if I were my dog and my dog were me; would I hop up in the bed and go fast asleep?

Would he sing to me waaay off key as I do him and see him look of me as I sing to him? What if I were my dog and my dog were me?

When we drive to work and he hops out to play all day with his doggy friends, does he think of me like I do him and hope his fun will never end?

I love you Shazam and thank you for all I am today, I am better than I was before and it's because of you I get better everyday to make sure to get closer to giving you the love you would give me if I were you and you were me.

Now, I hope that you enjoyed the love of Shazam and thoughts of the family pet in your home. On the next page we will begin a story. I will help you write your very own story about your family pet.

Your Preface Notes

Why are you writing this book?

What makes you believe in this idea and why others need to read your book?

Why is your family pet special to you?

What joy did you get writing about your family pet?

What do you want others to get from reading your book about your family pet?

Title

What if I were _____ and
_____ were me?

Your Family Pet's Picture, possibly
with you/and/or your family

By: _____   _____

Preface

I am writing this book to reflect in years to come about how I went to school in _____ _____. During this time, the entire world was experiencing a

_____.
My _____ gives me great joy that I would like to _____ with the _____. My mom loves me my _____ since _____. I do not agree with her, maybe when you read this book you can decide if I am right?

_____

_____

_____

_____

_____

If I were my _____ and my _____ were me, how would easy would my life be? No school, no _____. If I were _____ and he were me!!! All the dentist bills would not be orthodontist, they would be bills for the _____.

What if I were my _____ and my _____ were me? How much fun would that be? Would _____ eat my shoes or sleep in my _____.

Picture

Picture

We are so very lucky to have

_____.

S/he is so very special because s/he

_____

_____.

If my _____ were me and I
were s/he _____.

Picture

Picture

Would my mom love _____
more, or would my sister _____
_____ me more? What would it be if my
_____ were me and I were s/
he? Would s/he pull my ears, or would I pull
theirs? Would I sit on the bed or on the
counter? Would I _____

_____

_____

_____

Picture

Thank you for reading my book. I am hoping that you had as much fun reading it as _____

_____

_____

_____

_____

_____

_____

_____

_____

My hope is that you have been inspired to share something pleasant with the world during this pandemic.

Now that you have read one book and helped to write another. You are going to write your own book about whatever you, your Educator and/parental guardian agree upon for the last segment of this book.

Title

By:

Preface

_____

_____

_____

_____

_____

_____

_____

_____

Picture

Picture

Picture

Picture

30

Picture

Picture

32

If you are the parent or leader that supported the work of your learner. Thank you. evaluation of this work:

Creativity counts for 25 points _____

Organizational Thought 25 points _____

Spelling 25 points _____

Grammar points _____

Printed in the United States
by Baker & Taylor Publisher Services